The TotalCourage! Institute Playbook

The TotalCourage! Institute Playbook

Winning With Character

World Class Character Training for Your Team

First Edition

DEE DAUGHERTY
KENNETH MARFILIUS

ISBN-13: 9781533066244
ISBN-10: 1533066248

Table of Contents

Praise for

THE **TOTALCOURAGE! INSTITUTE** PLAYBOOK

"TotalCourage and its *Playbook* could not be more appropriate in the current climate of the digital age and given the inappropriate conduct by some student athletes and coaches. The *Playbook* gets right to the heart of the problem with life-changing solutions. A fantastic tool to teach and reinforce character."

—LARRY IVY, FORMER ATHLETIC DIRECTOR, UNIVERSITY OF KENTUCKY

"TotalCourage is a powerful program that motivates young individuals to lead a life of intentionality and good moral character."

—BERNADETTE MATTOX, FORMER DIVISION I NCAA HEAD BASKETBALL COACH AND WNBA COACH

"Every coach should have this playbook as a tool to reinforce character. I find many similarities in my studies of Proverbs in the Old Testament of the Bible. Profound, hard-hitting, and absolutely necessary."

—JERRY GLANVILLE, FORMER NFL HEAD COACH, HOUSTON OILERS AND ATLANTA FALCONS

"TotalCourage has developed a curriculum to develop student athletes into empathetic and morally grounded individuals. The tools available in the *Playbook* reinforce proper character development."

—NICHOLAS McKINNON, MD, ADULT, ADOLESCENT, AND GERIATRIC PSYCHIATRIST

THE TOTALCOURAGE! INSTITUTE PLAYBOOK

Preface

Our youth require reinforcement on the absolute necessity of leading a principled life in the digital age. Our behaviors, our thoughts, and even our images of the world around us are indelibly recorded in perpetuity by all of the social media options available to our youth. This amazing playbook was originally designed to focus on student-athletes at the high school, college, and university levels.

Children today follow their favorite athletes. However, the children today have access to immediate and detailed information on these role models, who are not much older than they are, and their influence, be it good or bad, is compelling.

We believe that this playbook can be used across the entire spectrum of our society to empower supervisors, instructors, and facilitators to lead vital discussions surrounding the necessity of comprehending and applying these character traits. However, this playbook is written in a way that an individual athlete, student, or employee can self-guide his or her own journey to a winning life of character. The reward in life is in the finish. We all move at a different pace, and if we are truly the sum of our life experiences, then these character traits can guide us to lead a more fruitful, responsible, and meaningful life.

It takes **TotalCourage!** to lead a life of character when surrounded by bad examples and undaunted peer pressure 24/7. These character traits have carried the esteemed members of our organization to the very heights of measurable success on and off the battlefield, in Fortune 500 companies, major universities, and on the field of play at the collegiate and professional levels.

This playbook is intended to be more than a coffee-table piece. It is a living document that is constantly being refined and updated with a single purpose of teaching young men and women to incorporate character in all aspects of their own life stories.

Our goal is to build an unbreakable chain of character traits that provides a continuous stream of consciousness surrounding leading a principled life. Situationally, more than one trait will be used to assess, analyze, or act, and in some complex situations, all the traits are required to resolve issues or make the right decisions in life. Live your life story and create your own unique brand. We hope that you enjoy the journey, and we look forward to receiving your feedback as we take this journey with you.

Introduction

The **TotalCourage!** vision is to provide world class character training. We are committed to closing the moral divide witnessed daily in our society. Our coaching team has over 125 years of combined experience training and mentoring thousands of young men and women to lead their own lives with character. We lead by example. Our philosophy is to provide on-site character development coaching tailored to teach, train, and mentor coaches, students, and athletes to win with character.

Our **TotalCourage!** program emphasizes key traits that inspire athletes to lead a principled life:

- Character and Its Impact on Winning
- Selflessness
- Integrity
- Tact and Diplomacy
- Commitment
- Initiative
- Enthusiasm
- Humility
- Loyalty
- Emotional Maturity
- Gratitude
- Decisiveness
- Resilience
- Live Your Story

With **TotalCourage!** we hammer home the consequences of leading a life of disrespect, immoral behavior, or criminal conduct. Our team members have all been senior leaders in our respective disciplines. We have consistently built winning teams of excellence in the US Armed Forces, universities and colleges, and Fortune 500 corporations. Our success is based on leading a principled life of character.

Funded by individual donors, foundations, and corporate sponsors, **TotalCourage!** seeks to provide character training to high school and college athletic teams nationwide at no charge.

Acknowledgments

The authors wish to thank the entire **TotalCourage!** staff, their friends, and especially their families for their unyielding support. Warmest aloha to our board of directors for their patience and support. Of particular note, the authors thank the selfless coaches, teachers, and administrators who devote countless hours mentoring, caring for, and teaching our youth to lead principled lives.

1

Character and Its Impact on Winning

The members of the **TotalCourage!** team devoted all of their adult lives mentoring, coaching, and developing eighteen-to-twenty-five-year-old men and women to lead principled lives and to excel in the face of adversity.

What was the secret sauce that led these distinguished leaders to consistently create winning teams of highly principled young men and women? Virtually every day we see or hear in the news stories about coaches not leading by example or not being appropriate role models. Why? More alarming, we see tremendous young athletes throwing their futures away because of selfish behaviors: sexual assault, alcohol and drug abuse, taking performance-enhancing drugs (PEDs), racking up DUIs, engaging in theft or breaking and entering, and too many other misdemeanors and felonies to mention. Why?

Before we answer these questions, it is important to acknowledge that there are more coaches and athletes doing the right thing and doing things right every day as a silent majority.

One might ask why the members of **TotalCourage!** are inspired to single out coaches and athletes instead of society at large. The answer is quite simple, coaches and athletes are in the limelight, and children look up to them as role models. Some argue that coaches and athletes are perceived to be entitled, and they face many temptations that the mainstream public may not encounter.

Before we embark on this journey of **TotalCourage!** together, let's decide right now that electing to lead an unprincipled life of disrespect, immoral behavior, lies, or criminal conduct is, in a word, cowardly. We have choices in life. What is your choice?

Throughout the workbook you will be introduced to distinct character traits to gain insights and answers to these questions. You will take an inspiring journey into the meaning of character, and if applied, it will lead to a better life, a life of limitless possibilities, of happiness, and of confidence: a life of **TotalCourage!**

SOCIAL RESPONSIBILITY

We are excited to begin this journey of **TotalCourage!** with you! The next two sections should paint a picture of the importance of character development and character training for our youth.

Today, we hear a great deal about political correctness, and as a society we seem to be overly sensitive, or in some instances too cautious, when it comes to making the right choice or the right decision.

This playbook is about character, not politics. It is about doing the right thing and doing things right. It is about teaching responsibility and accountability. It is about resilience and understanding the importance of living your own life story.

As a nation we appear to be generally lacking in social responsibility. In order to fully be a person of character you must display common courtesy, justice, and judgment. These traits should be behavioral underpinnings as you embark on a life of **TotalCourage!**

Our society is changing rapidly in the digital age due to educational, legal, and social reforms. Increasingly, your teammates and you will be challenged to be socially responsible.

Social responsibility is the latest buzzword that the media and educators have latched onto in order to categorize appropriate behavior in the twenty-first century.

Social responsibility simply means to be aware of others and to appreciate that others have different faiths, behaviors, and beliefs. It means to apply common courtesy in dealing with others who differ from you or have different opinions, and it means applying fairness and good judgment in dealing with others who are different from you or whose beliefs differ from yours.

We live in a free society, and the rule of law requires us to be accepting of others. Our inalienable rights separate us from all other people on earth. Compared to most nations on earth, we are very fortunate.

Discrimination and bias based on one's race, faith, or orientation is simply not accepted in our society, and it is most definitely not accepted on your team.

Recently, a highly accomplished assistant coach for an NFL team approached a college athlete at the NFL Combine and questioned the athlete's sexual orientation, in addition to giving him his opinion about the perceived climate in his own organization.

The college athlete was mortified to be singled out this way when the NFL Combine is about athletic skill, character, and potential to fit into the scheme of one of thirty-two NFL teams. As we look at the coach who made this remark, he was an outstanding college and NFL athlete, and he is a fine family man devoted to his wife and children. Up to this point, he led his life above reproach.

Did he fail as a coach? Can he be forgiven? The answer is "yes" to both questions. His organization ensured that he was given in-depth social responsibility training and he was counseled in writing by his head coach on the importance of being sensitive to our transforming society.

He is now a fish in a fishbowl, being observed day and night by a society that is tolerating zero defects when it comes to social responsibility. Can he survive this mistake and have a fruitful coaching career? Of course! However, public opinion will not be kind to him if he makes the same mistake twice.

Display the **TotalCourage!** it takes to be emotionally mature and socially responsible. Be fair, be courteous, and use good judgment when speaking or behaving. Do the right thing, and do things right because it is simply the right thing to do! Your life will be more productive, less stressful, and happier!

Due to the digital age and the affordability and availability of smartphones, everything you say or do could potentially be recorded for all to see or hear. Data is stored on the Internet, and irresponsible conduct can be an albatross for the remainder of your life for all to see. Be an example of social responsibility on and off the field, and the rewards will be infinite.

ENDURANCE

The common thread throughout this playbook is **TotalCourage!** It takes more courage to lead a principled life than one of selfish behavior. A life of **TotalCourage!** takes endurance.

We define *endurance* as the physical, mental, spiritual, and emotional willpower to overcome pain, adversity, suffering, or defeat. Endurance defines true men and women of character.

We will discuss many inviolable character traits, but endurance is the high-tempered steel that comprises the unbreakable chain of **TotalCourage!** Each link requires stamina to break through your own pain threshold, or to stretch your mind to accept and learn new concepts, or to have the patience to rely on your faith, or the maturity it takes to be resolute when others are weak.

In this playbook, we talk a lot about differentiating yourself from others in a world where everyone has a common base of knowledge due to access to the Internet, but it is much deeper than that! Our nation requires leadership at every level.

Arguably, one of the toughest character traits to master is physical courage. How do you train your brain to say *go*, when your body says *no*? Olympic rowers often discuss breaking through the pain threshold. Soldiers and marines are all too familiar with that concept. You are not expected to like pain, but accepting the inevitability of pain in training and competition is a given.

We do not have to look very far to find amazing examples of physical courage in our own walk of life. Mental and physical toughness are the calling cards of true warriors. Fight through the pain, be humble, be determined, be resolute, and never quit. However, physical courage is more than acceptance of unendurable conditions, it is also enduring pain without complaining. Have the **TotalCourage!** to withstand the pain and lift others up while doing so.

In an increasingly "me" oriented society, our teams, businesses, schools, and communities need leaders with the endurance required to be role models that uphold goodness, empathy, compassion, and action!

Reach deep within yourself and find the endurance to overcome all obstacles while winning with character. Now, roll up your sleeves as you blast into this curriculum en route to a more rewarding life!

TOTALCOURAGE! PLEDGE

Before we get started, take some personal time to reflect. How do you plan to live a principled life of **TotalCourage!** What is your choice? In your own words, use the space provided below to answer the questions and take the pledge!

_____

_____

_____

_____

_____

_____

_____

_____

_____

_____

_____

_____

_____

2

Selflessness

The foundation of character

This chapter is dedicated to the foundation of character, in a word, selflessness. Throughout our lives, our parents, guardians, and coaches have led us to believe that integrity, or being honest with oneself first and honest with others always, is the foundation of character. At **TotalCourage!** we believe that integrity is the first pillar that holds up the roof of character, but being selfless in every act and deed is the foundation upon which all other character traits stand.

All that we have to do is read the newspaper, watch sports channels, look at our smartphone applications, or peruse the Internet, and we see trouble practically every day. We see coaches and athletes making selfish decisions that affect not only themselves and their families but their entire team and the institutions they represent.

Topics such as sexual assault, alcohol and drug abuse, theft, and immoral or indecent behavior can be seen as cowardly and selfish acts.

- Are these selfish acts done only because of selfish motivation?
- Are they committed because of temptation?
- Are they done due to peer pressure?
- Some may even claim that they did not know the difference between right and wrong.

Friends, if there is any doubt that a behavior might be right or wrong, then don't do it! A selfless leader, a selfless teammate, a selfless citizen doesn't put himself or herself in a position to be questioned.

The consequences of selfish behavior not only alienate the person who acted selfishly, but they create dissension and divisiveness on a team or in an organization. If you can't be a winner in life, you cannot consistently win on the field, period.

Selflessness...

- ...is about putting others before yourself.
- ...is about giving credit to others.
- ...is about humility, which we will discuss later.
- ...in the final assessment is about caring.

If you truly want to improve your life, your team, and your future, you must reach deep into your heart and exhibit a caring attitude toward others.

A caring leader and a caring teammate always looks at the second and third order effects of any decision. How will this decision be perceived by my teammates?

Selflessness begins and ends with caring. Ask yourself if you are placing your own success, desires, or ambitions above that of your team, your family, or friends. Reflect on how much you care about them and how you can modify your behavior to lift others up, and then consider how your priorities mesh with your team's priorities. Your team comes first.

Be selfless and you can expect immediate rewards in your life on and off the field!

TOTALCOURAGE! LESSON PLAN & ACTIVITY
Lesson objective:

Guide students to...

- ...define the character trait of selflessness.
- ...see selflessness in their lives.
- ...apply and develop the principle of selflessness personally.
- ...engage in both large and small group discussions about selflessness.

1. **Formal *Merriam-Webster* Definition of *Selflessness*:**
   Selflessness: having or showing great concern for other people and little or no concern for yourself.
2. **Total Courage! Definition of *Selflessness*:**
   The foundation of character. Being selfless in every act and every deed is the foundation upon which all other character traits stand. Selflessness begins and ends with caring.
3. **Please provide your personal definition of *selflessness*:**

   _____

   _____

   _____

4. **Case Presentation**

   The following case example is based on a true story. However, names have been withheld for confidentiality purposes.

   In 2003, an army patrol was ambushed. The soldiers were National Guardsmen from Las Vegas, New Mexico. The driver of the truck was shot through the shoulder, and the passenger kicked open the door at twenty-five miles per hour, he selflessly stood up on the running board, and fired back with his M-16, dispatching two enemy assailants. He, too, was wounded, but after medical treatment both soldiers returned to duty. Just before the soldiers were decorated with Purple Hearts, the shooter was asked by his commander what he did for a living back in New Mexico. He replied, "Sir, I am an anger management specialist with the Bureau of Indian Affairs." The profound message is that he was an American citizen trained to diffuse conflict and violence in his civilian role, but he quickly reacted selflessly to protect his teammate at the risk of his own life.

5. **Small-Group Breakout Session**

   Interview your partner and record his/her responses to be shared with the group

   Keeping in mind the above definitions of *selflessness*, how does the above case example demonstrate the character trait of selflessness to you?

   _____

   _____

   _____

   _____

   Can you provide an example of a time in your life when you have been a caring leader or teammate and looked at the second and third order effects of your decisions?

   _____

   _____

_____

_____

_____

After learning about what it means to be selfless, how do you plan to improve your life, your team, and your future?

_____

_____

_____

_____

_____

6. **Group Discussion:** Each team, or small group, will present their partners' answers to the above interview questions, and we will form a collective meaning of *self-lessness*. Please use the space below to write the agreed-upon collective meaning of the character trait selflessness.

_____

_____

_____

_____

_____

TOTALCOURAGE! JOURNAL

Please answer the following questions prior to our next session. This journal entry will serve as a reminder of how to live a life of selflessness and ultimately a life of **TotalCourage!**

In 140 characters or less, please describe what living a life of selflessness means to you.

_____

_____

_____

_____

_____

Have you modified your behaviors to lift others up since completing the lesson on selflessness?

_____

_____

_____

_____

_____

Social Media Suggestion
Those who wish to use social media instead of writing in a journal can tweet their thoughts to **@totalcourage** using the hashtag *#selflessness*.

3

Integrity

The ability to do the right thing when no one is watching

If selflessness is the foundation of character, then the first pillar that holds up the roof of character is integrity.

We determined that in order to be completely selfless, one must care about oneself but more importantly about others. *Integrity* is defined very simply as being honest with oneself first and then honest with others always. This is a tall task. But if you want to lead a life of character, honesty is nonnegotiable.

Virtually every day, we see athletes who make selfish decisions that affect the outcome of not only the next game but in some instances the entire season. For example, a quarterback was suspended for an entire calendar year after it was determined by the NCAA that he selfishly used a banned performance-enhancing drug. The entire team suffered the consequences. His lack of integrity affected his entire team and their chances for a possible conference and/or national championship.

Being honest is a selfless act…lying is selfish. The best teams, organizations, churches, and businesses are those that have a climate of selflessness and integrity. The most important aspect when faced with character faults of a teammate is to display the courage to never pass a mistake. Calmly and professionally address the issue of integrity with the individual first. If that fails, go to your team captain or coach and share the selfish act or lack of integrity that you witnessed.

Lying is a cancer, and the only way to heal it on a winning team is to hold the individual or individuals accountable as quickly as possible. Accountability and responsibility to say and do what is right regardless of the consequences defines character. Remember this: it is easier to do the right thing and to do things right than it is to take shortcuts, deceive, lie, or put your own personal interests above those of your teammates. Display the **TotalCourage!** it takes to be a winner.

TOTALCOURAGE! LESSON PLAN & ACTIVITY
Lesson objective:

Guide students to…

- …define the character trait of integrity.
- …see integrity in their lives.
- …apply and develop the principle of integrity personally.
- …engage in both large and small group discussions about integrity.

1. **Formal *Merriam-Webster* Definition of *Integrity***
   Integrity: firm adherence to a code of especially moral values.
2. **TotalCourage! Definition of *Integrity*:**
   Integrity is defined very simply as being honest with oneself first and then honest with others always.
3. **Please provide your personal definition of *integrity*:**

_____

_____

_____

4. **Presentation:**

Please read the following case example and answer the corresponding questions on the following page.

Julie, a top student athlete on the women's basketball team had been drinking with her friends throughout the evening. The party was wrapping up, and she decided she did not want to call a cab and leave her vehicle overnight. She told her friends that she'd had only one drink and was sober. Julie, continuing to be dishonest with her friends, decided to get behind the wheel after having had more than six drinks over the course of three hours. On the drive home, she clipped another vehicle, breaking the mirror. She stopped momentarily to see if anyone had witnessed the accident. After seeing no one in the vicinity, she proceeded to drive her vehicle home, parking it in the driveway. Fortunately, Julie arrived home safely. She would never be questioned for hitting another vehicle, and no one was aware of her driving while impaired. The next morning she attended her basketball practice as if nothing had happened.

5. **Personal Reflection**

    Please take some time to reflect on the following questions and provide your answers below.

    Let's revisit Julie's situation. If you were presented with this dilemma, what decision would you have made? If *integrity* is defined very simply as, "being honest with oneself first and then honest with others always," then what are the potential second and third order effects of Julie's decisions?

    _____

    _____

    _____

    _____

    _____

    Keeping in mind your personal definition of *integrity*, can you think of a time in your life when you did not abide by your personal values and views on the concept of integrity?

    _____

    _____

    _____

    _____

    _____

What steps do you plan to take in your own life to hold yourself accountable? Do you have the moral courage to do what is right regardless of the consequences? Do you see why integrity and moral courage are complementary? Briefly explain why.

_____

_____

_____

_____

_____

6. **Small-Group Discussion**

    Take some time to reflect on those who have led their lives based on integrity. Please select one individual that you believe embodies a life based on integrity, and provide a description of that individual below. This individual can be a role model, mentor, coach, relative, or public figure. Upon completion, please share your answers with your team member(s).

    Name: _____

    Description of individual:

    _____

    _____

    _____

    _____

    _____

Why do you believe this individual embodies a life based on integrity?

_____

_____

_____

_____

_____

TOTALCOURAGE! JOURNAL

This journal entry will serve as a reminder of how to live a life of integrity and ultimately a life of **TotalCourage!**

Please take a picture of the person you have identified above as living a life of integrity, including a caption. If you are unable to take a picture, please provide an old photo, or photo provided from the Internet. If unable to obtain a photo of the aforementioned individual, use this space below to describe how you plan to emulate the individual's integrity in your own life.

Social Media Suggestion
Those who wish to use social media instead of writing in a journal can tweet their thoughts to **@totalcourage** using the hashtag *#integrity*.

4

Tact and Diplomacy

How to apply patience and consideration of others by applying tact and diplomacy in all aspects of your life

In our previous lessons, we tackled some pretty heavy issues. We discussed the need to display **TotalCourage!** in your life both on and off the field and the value and consequences of doing so. We have discussed selflessness and integrity and the moral courage it takes to lead a principled life.

In this lesson, let's take the time to discuss the courage it takes to apply patience and consideration of others by using tact and diplomacy in all aspects of your life. It is not disrespectful to disagree provided you use tact and timing. Nor is it acceptable to never pass a mistake, but you have to know when and how to address that mistake.

Yelling at and confronting others in public has very little positive effect. In fact, it often results in a negative response. The best approach to dealing with conflict, correcting others, or addressing issues of dishonesty, selfishness, and bad behavior overall is to pull a person or people aside and address them calmly regarding the consequences of their bad decisions. Sensitivity and thoughtfulness in dealing with others, especially when addressing difficult issues that can affect the performance of an individual or an entire team, are most effective. Don't shoot, then aim…take a deep breath, pull the individual(s) aside, be considerate, and correct their mistakes.

The essence of teamwork is consideration of others when adversity is the norm rather than the rule. Display the **TotalCourage!** it takes to use tact, diplomacy, and proper timing in handling conflict. Remember, your reputation is what other people think about you, but your character is who you are when no one is looking. Lead a principled life, and your example will be infectious.

TOTALCOURAGE! LESSON PLAN & ACTIVITY
Lesson objective:

Guide students to…

- …define the character traits of tact and diplomacy.
- …see tact and diplomacy in their lives.
- …apply and develop the principles of tact and diplomacy personally.
- …engage in both large and small group discussions about tact and diplomacy

1. **Formal *Merriam-Webster* Definition of *Tact* and *Diplomacy***
   Tact: the ability to do or say things without offending or upsetting people.
   Diplomacy: skill in dealing with others without causing bad feelings.
2. **TotalCourage! Definition of *Tact* and *Diplomacy***
   The courage it takes to apply patience and consideration of others.
3. **Please provide your personal definition of *tact* and *diplomacy*:**

_____

_____

_____

4. Case Presentation

Please read the case example below, and provide your response to the corresponding questions on the following page.

Jason, one of your fellow teammates, decided to go out drinking the night before the big game. Several of Jason's friends outside of the team informed you that he was with them late into the night. You have also viewed pictures on the Internet of Jason partying with bottles of alcohol.

The game is the next afternoon, and you decide that it is better just to play the game and avoid any conflict. Jason is a starter on the team and has one of the worst performances of the season. After the game, you quietly confront Jason, and he adamantly denies that staying up late and consuming alcohol with his drinking buddies had an adverse effect on his game performance. You are the only member of the team who has been informed of Jason's behaviors. The coach just wrapped up the postgame talk and has departed the locker room while all members of the team are still present in the locker room. Keeping in mind today's lesson on tact and diplomacy, "having the courage it takes to apply patience and consideration of others," please answer the following questions.

5. **Individual Exercise**

   Please answer the questions below before proceeding to the small-group exercise.

   If you were presented with this scenario in your own life, how would you react?

   _____

   _____

   _____

   _____

   What is the best approach to dealing with this conflict?

   _____

   _____

   _____

   Would you address the behavior(s)? If so, how would you address Jason and his decision to stay up late and consume alcohol the night prior to the game?

   _____

   _____

   _____

   _____

6. Small-Group Breakout Session

Please pair up and compare your answers with your partner's. Remember, it is not disrespectful to disagree provided you use tact and timing.

Please use the space below to compare and contrast the team's response. Work with your partner to come up with a collective answer(s) to the questions above, and be prepared to share with the group.

_____

_____

_____

_____

_____

TOTALCOURAGE! JOURNAL

Over the course of the next week, select one instance in which you have witnessed or personally displayed an act of tact and diplomacy.

_____

_____

_____

_____

_____

Please describe why you believe this example is appropriate and how it displays the **TotalCourage!** it takes to use tact, diplomacy, and proper timing in handling conflict.

_____

_____

_____

_____

_____

Social Media Suggestion
Students who wish to use social media instead of writing in a journal can tweet their thoughts to **@totalcourage** using the hashtag *#Tact&Diplomacy*.

5

Commitment

Have a plan, work smart, and stay committed!

Thus far we have discussed selflessness, integrity, tact and diplomacy, and the responsibility it takes to never ignore a mistake. These traits are all essential ingredients to becoming a person or a team of character.

In this lesson we will stress the importance of commitment and knowledge. Life is a one-way trip. We are placed here to maximize our gifts and our potential every single day. Commitment and hard work defined by a selfless drive for excellence means nothing if you don't work smart, as well.

Commitment and *knowledge* are synonymous when defining a person or a team with character. If you are truly focused on your goals as you strive for excellence, then you must study the best practices, and the best techniques and methodologies, so that you can instinctively apply them to achieving success at the height of the competition. Speed, agility, and strength are vital for an athlete, but technical and practical knowledge enable you to better prepare and separate yourself from your opponent.

Determination, motivation, enthusiasm, and guts are all required to be fully committed, but you have to have a plan, you have to work smart, and you must be a student of your desires. One must reach deep inside oneself and be fully committed in order to achieve excellence.

Be committed, stay committed, and seek knowledge. Regardless of the score, you will always be a winner. Apply the **TotalCourage!** it takes to be truly committed to excellence. Don't allow self-doubt to creep in, or temptation, or distractions to dissuade you from commitment. Rise above! Work hard! Work smart!

Lastly, remember that a bad attitude only hurts the person with the bad attitude. A totally committed individual makes the best teammate because that individual arrives every day with a positive attitude in the pursuit of excellence.

TOTALCOURAGE! LESSON PLAN & ACTIVITY
Lesson objective:

Guide students to…

- …define the character trait of commitment.
- …see commitment in their lives.
- …apply and develop the principle of commitment personally.
- …engage in both large and small group discussions about commitment.

1. **Formal *Merriam-Webster* Definition of *Commitment***
   Commitment:
   - a promise to do or give something.
   - a promise to be loyal to someone or something.
   - attitude of someone who works very hard to do or support something.

2. **TotalCourage! Definition of *Commitment*:**
   A selfless drive for excellence combining hard work and knowledge to achieve your goals!

3. **Please provide your personal definition of *commitment*:**

   _____

   _____

   _____

4. **Case Presentation**

    Please utilize the space below to present your own case example of commitment. Referring back to your pledge on page 3, have you remained committed to a life of **TotalCourage!**? In your writing, please consider incorporating the character traits we have already discussed. Have you remained loyal to living a life of self-lessness, integrity, tact, and diplomacy? If not, how do you plan to reverse the trend and promise to be a totally committed individual to yourself and to those around you? Your writing should provide personal examples. Please be prepared to share your examples with the group.

    _____

    _____

    _____

    _____

    _____

    _____

    _____

5. **Small-Group Breakout Session**

   Please interview your team partner on the following questions:

   How did you feel when you were completing the exercise? Did you remain honest and loyal to yourself?

   _____

   _____

   Was it difficult having to challenge yourself on whether or not you have stayed committed to character traits we have discussed in previous lessons?

   _____

   _____

6. **Group Discussion**

   What is one way you can remind yourself on a daily basis to be committed, stay committed, and seek knowledge? After hearing suggestions from the group, please list the top three reminders you believe will be most helpful.

   1. _____

   2. _____

   3. _____

TOTALCOURAGE! JOURNAL

The **TotalCourage!** team believes that a totally committed individual makes the best teammate because that individual arrives every day with a positive attitude toward the pursuit of excellence. Use your top three reminders on the previous page to assist you in arriving every day with a positive attitude.

Please provide an explanation below on how these reminders have assisted you in your journey toward becoming a totally committed individual.

_____

_____

_____

Continually seeking knowledge is part of staying committed. How do you plan to refine your skill-set on a daily basis, contributing to a life of excellence?

_____

_____

_____

Social Media Suggestion
Those who wish to use social media instead of writing in a journal can tweet their thoughts to **@totalcourage** using the hashtag *#commitment*.

6

Initiative

Don't wait for your ship to come in; swim out to it!

Initiative plus improvement equals success. In the past couple of lessons, we have spoken about the need to never ignore a mistake. It takes a measure of moral courage and commitment to face the transgressions of others. As we also discussed, it requires timing and tact to approach a teammate who isn't giving 100 percent or who is not leading a principled life. In that vein, we would like to emphasize the value of initiative as a character trait that requires **TotalCourage!**

Thus far, we have touched upon inviolable character traits such as selflessness, integrity, tact and diplomacy, and commitment. But what is initiative? Simply defined, it is positive action to do things right and to do the right thing without being told or when no one is looking.

A highly decorated military officer once said, "In the absence of orders, attack!" In other words, if there is a job to be done and you understand the intent and you have the resources, then don't wait around to be told what to do. Get the job done, and do it right the first time. Remember, we said in the very beginning that selflessness is the foundation of character.

If you are truly selfless, then initiative comes naturally. *Initiative* is synonymous with *improvement* because action is always better than inaction. You can have all of the character traits in the world, but without initiative you cannot apply those traits.

Winning teams are on-time, every time. When the coaches blow the final whistle at practice, who stays behind for an extra fifteen minutes to improve? Take the initiative to continually improve and to never ignore a mistake. Seize the initiative when nobody is looking, and don't worry about who gets the credit. Display the **TotalCourage!** to ramp it up a notch and succeed. Don't ever wait around to be told what to do.

TOTALCOURAGE! LESSON PLAN & ACTIVITY

Lesson objective:

Guide students to…

- …define the character trait of initiative.
- …see initiative in their lives.
- …apply and develop the principle of initiative personally.
- …engage in both large and small group discussions about initiative.

1. **Formal *Merriam-Webster* Definition of *Initiative*:**
   Initiative: the ability to assess and initiate things independently.
2. **TotalCourage! Definition of *Initiative*:**
   The positive action to do things right and to do the right thing without being told or when no one is looking.
3. **Please provide your personal definition of *initiative*:**

   _____

   _____

   _____

4. Case Presentation

Please read the following case example and respond to the corresponding questions.

Melinda and Chris met during their freshman year of college and have been friends for four years. Melinda and Chris are in the final few months of their senior year and out of their competitive seasons. They have decided to "live it up" and party on the weekends. While at a party, Chris noticed Melinda beginning to slur her words, and she appeared unsteady on her feet. Several hours later, Chris witnesses several men talking to Melinda on the couch in the back room. Chris, noticing his friend intoxicated and seemingly unaware of what is unfolding, decides to casually walk by the group on the couch. At first glance, he notices one of the men mocking Melinda and taking pictures with her for Snapchat. Chris, not wanting to make a scene, retrieves one of Melinda's close friends, telling her what he has witnessed. Chris and Melinda's close friend decide to get Melinda and leave the party immediately.

5. Small-Group Breakout Session

Interview your partner and record his/her responses to be shared with the group

Upon reading the case, what thoughts were going through your mind?

_____

_____

_____

_____

How did Chris take initiative? What did Chris's selfless act potentially prevent?

_____

_____

_____

What could some of the potential consequences have been if Chris had not displayed the character traits of selflessness, integrity, tact and diplomacy, commitment, and ultimately initiative?

_____

_____

_____

6. **Group Discussion:** At **TotalCourage!** we believe that *initiative* is synonymous with *improvement* because action is always better than inaction. You can have all of the character traits in the world, but without initiative you cannot apply those traits, modeling them for others. Expanding upon the questions and answers above, think critically about the decision-making process throughout the scenario. Have you ever encountered a similar scenario? If so, how did/would you react to a similar situation?

As you listen to the group's discussion, please use the space below to take notes on how Initiative + Improvement= Success in your life. We will talk more about initiative in Chapter 12.

_____

_____

_____

_____

_____

_____

_____

_____

TOTALCOURAGE! JOURNAL

Please answer the following questions prior to our next session. This journal entry will serve as a reminder of how to live a life of initiative and ultimately a life of **TotalCourage!**

Over the course of the next few days, make a conscious effort to do the right thing, without being told and when no one is looking. For your private use, use the space below to write down the positive action you took when no one was looking.

_____

_____

_____

_____

We all witness people taking initiative every day. When you witness such an act, you are being challenged to bring out the good in people and thank them for living a principled life. In place of this journal entry, you can take a picture with this individual and post it to Instagram with the hashtag *#initiative*. Be sure to provide a description of the act and tag **@totalcourage** in an effort to spread your positive message of living a principled life.

_____

_____

_____

_____

Social Media Suggestion
Those who wish to use social media instead of writing in a journal can tweet their thoughts to **@totalcourage** using the hashtag *#initiative*.

7

Enthusiasm

Be passionate and create your own enthusiasm.

Not everybody is a cheerleader. However, if you want to be a person of character, and if you want to be a valued teammate, then enthusiasm is a trait you cannot ignore. Enthusiasm wells up from the heart, and it is an infectious component of being a winner. You don't have to always be vocal, but you can display enthusiasm in other ways.

In our last lesson, we talked about the importance of taking action over inaction and how important initiative is as a character trait. When faced with adversity, the glass can be half-full or half-empty. It is your choice.

Remember, in previous lessons, we spoke about attitude. A bad attitude only hurts the person with the bad attitude in the end. Enthusiasm defined in this context simply means being positive. Display your positivity and your excitement, and it will spread throughout your team.

Enthusiasm combined with challenges or adversity makes work feel easy. Problems are easier to solve, and victories are easier to achieve when all are working toward a common goal with a positive attitude and genuine heartfelt excitement. Enthusiasm breeds success because it makes oneself and others believe that no mission is too difficult.

Display the **TotalCourage!** it takes to believe, to be positive, and to be excited. Roman warriors chanted "*carpe diem*" in formation each morning. Seize the day! Be selfless—do it for yourself and others.

TOTALCOURAGE! LESSON PLAN & ACTIVITY

Lesson objective:

Guide students to…

- …define the character trait of enthusiasm.
- …see initiative in their lives.
- …apply and develop the principle of enthusiasm personally.
- …engage in both large and small group discussions about enthusiasm.

1. **Formal *Merriam-Webster* Definition of *Enthusiasm***
   Enthusiasm: strong excitement about something: a strong feeling of active interest in something that you like or enjoy.
2. **Total Courage! Definition of *Enthusiasm***
   Enthusiasm defined in this context, simply means "to be consistently positive in your words, acts, and deeds, when things are going well and in the face of adversity."
3. **Please provide your personal definition of *enthusiasm*:**

_____

_____

_____

4. Case Presentation

Amanda was not highly recruited out of high school for softball. However, she dreamed of becoming a Division I athlete. Prior to attending the Division I institution, she trained endlessly with her high school coaches. Eventually, Amanda would attend walk-on tryouts and was selected for the final roster spot. The coach stated, "with her hustle, heart, and desire, she brings an added emotional dimension to this team that we need." Amanda would end up playing all four years and would earn a scholarship her junior and senior years. She never missed a practice, game, or extra workout. However, she also only played in one game during her entire four-year career. This game would be played in her senior year. As Amanda walked up to the plate, all of her teammates, coaches, athletic trainers, and fans stood to their feet and chanted her name. Amanda and her coach participated in the postgame interview. Amanda thanked her coaching staff and teammates for giving her the opportunity to be part of a special community, and she is now a lifetime supporter. Amanda's coach quickly responded with, "No, thank you! You have been an invaluable asset to our program, and you have taught us all so much about 'bringing it' every day, with a positive attitude and genuine excitement for the love of the game and mostly for the love of those around you."

5. **Personal Reflection**

How did Amanda's enthusiasm contribute to the team environment?

_____

_____

_____

Do you believe that attitude and positivity breed success? If so, how?

_____

_____

_____

Can you think of a valued teammate who has displayed enthusiasm? What makes this individual stand out?

_____

_____

_____

How are enthusiasm and commitment complementary? Explain.

_____

_____

_____

6. **Group Discussion**

   At **TotalCourage!** we believe that when you display positivity and excitement, it becomes contagious and spreads throughout the team.

   Keeping in mind the answers to your questions above, can you provide the group with an example of how you or your team overcame adversity through enthusiasm and a positive attitude?

   _____

   _____

   _____

   _____

   _____

   _____

   _____

   _____

TOTALCOURAGE! JOURNAL

Please answer the following questions prior to our next session. This journal entry will serve as a reminder of how to live a life of enthusiasm and ultimately a life of **TotalCourage!**

Over the course of the next few days, make a conscious effort to infuse enthusiasm into your words, acts, and deeds. Be an inspiration to others! Use the space below to write down an example of how you infused enthusiasm into your own life.

_____

_____

_____

_____

We all witness people displaying enthusiasm every day. In place of this journal entry, you can take or find a video of someone displaying enthusiasm and post it to social media with the hashtag *#enthusiasm*. Be sure to provide a description of the act and tag **@totalcourage** in an effort to spread your positive message of living a principled life.

_____

_____

_____

_____

Social Media Suggestion
Those who wish to use social media instead of writing in a journal can tweet their thoughts to **@totalcourage** using the hashtag *#enthusiasm*.

8

Humility

Treat others how you want to be treated

In this lesson, we will discuss the absolute necessity to approach your life with humility. *Humility*, simply defined, is that quiet confidence and inner strength required to be a true person of character.

In many cases we see bad examples of athletes who have allowed their ego to cloud better judgment. Find the **TotalCourage!** to be humble. We live in a culture in which we place great importance on being number one. What we fail to understand is that being number one is fleeting, and nobody can stay at the top all the time. Somebody will come along who is bigger, faster, stronger, and smarter. That is a constant in life.

Strive to be the best because you were blessed with many gifts and because you should maximize those gifts every single day. When you win, do it with dignity and humility. Give your family, friends, coaches, and teammates the credit. I assure you that the rewards will come back to you for a lifetime. There is no need to brag, insult, cajole, talk smack, or harass your opponent when they're beaten. Have the **TotalCourage!** to pick your opponent up, shake their hand, and tell them that they did a good job. Remember, even the greatest athletes and the greatest teams have a bad day.

Follow the Golden Rule and treat others how you want to be treated. Humility is the underlying component of self-respect. Without humility, it is impossible to respect others. Find the **TotalCourage!** to rise above immature, disrespectful, and outlandish behavior toward your opponent. Take the high ground. Be humble. Humble people are the most teachable people.

Humble teammates are the most coachable teammates. When you're listening, you're learning. When you are learning, you are improving. Be humble.

TOTALCOURAGE! LESSON PLAN & ACTIVITY

Lesson objective:

Guide students to…

- …define the character trait of humility.
- …see humility in their lives.
- …apply and develop the principle of humility personally.
- …engage in both large and small group discussions about humility.

1. **Formal *Merriam-Webster* Definition of *Humility***
   Humility: the quality or state of not thinking you are better than other people: the quality or state of being humble.
2. **TotalCourage! Definition of *Humility*:**
   Humility, simply defined, is that quiet confidence and inner strength required to be a true person of character.
3. **Please provide your personal definition of *humility*:**

_____

_____

_____

4. **Case Presentation**

   The film is presented by ESPN Films 30 for 30 Shorts. It is titled *Student/Athlete* and directed by Ken Jeong. The film is about a student athlete named Reggie Ho. Reggie Ho enrolled at Notre Dame hoping to pursue a career in medicine. But he also made history as a walk-on kicker who helped the Irish win a National Championship in 1988.

   For this next presentation, we will present a film. Please go to the following link in your classroom or on your smartphones. (It is less than 14 minutes long.)

   https://www.youtube.com/watch?v=30YrZCTNobQ

5. **Small-Group Breakout Session**

   Please pair up and interview your partner asking the following questions:

   Can you tell me what *humility* means to you?

   _____

   _____

   _____

   _____

   Can you provide one example of how you display humility in your own life?

   _____

   _____

   _____

   _____

Can you provide one example of how you have witnessed humility play out in the lives of others?

_____

_____

_____

_____

6. **Group Discussion:** Each team will present their partners' answers to the above interview questions, and we will form a collective meaning of _humility_.

_____

_____

_____

_____

TOTALCOURAGE! JOURNAL

Please answer the following questions prior to our next session. This journal entry will serve as a reminder of how to live a life of humility and ultimately a life of **TotalCourage!**

How can you implement the character trait of humility in your everyday life?

_____

_____

_____

_____

What have you done differently in your life since our lesson on humility?

_____

_____

_____

_____

Social Media Suggestion
Those who wish to use social media instead of writing in a journal can tweet their thoughts to **@totalcourage** using the hashtag *#humility*.

9

Loyalty

Lead by example.

We have covered a lot of territory over the last few lessons together. It is our hope that you are applying these character traits and examples in your own life and that you are becoming a better person.

It takes **TotalCourage!** to lead a principled life, and each lesson is a building block for you to construct a happy life of character. The rewards and gifts are immeasurable, and they last a lifetime.

In this lesson we are going to discuss loyalty as it applies to character. Defined, *loyalty* means, "being true and faithful to your organization, your team, your coaches, and your teammates," but not always in that order.

Loyalty is a multidirectional, multilayered trait that can either lift you up or destroy you. Being true to and supporting those around you can only happen in a climate of mutual respect and trust. Loyalty in a climate of selfishness, lies, and bad behavior will ruin your team and you.

The **TotalCourage!** founder and character coach Dee Daugherty stated the following in regards to his time on the front lines, "If you talk to combat veterans who have witnessed prolonged violent action, they will tell you that, above all things, they were most loyal to the guy to the left and to the right of them. That does not mean they were not loyal to the Constitution, to their commanders, or to their other teammates. On the contrary, it simply means that when the bullets were flying, their greatest loyalty was to the guy next to them. As a coach and as a commander of troops in battle, I can tell you without hesitation that my loyalty was always directed to the guys and gals at the tip of the spear. My commanders above me knew this, and they respected me for it."

Your coaches obviously want you to be honest, respectful, and supportive of their goals and leadership philosophy. However, they expect you to have your buddy's back both on and off the field. They expect you to be loyal and never pass a mistake. They expect you to lead by example. They expect you to mentor your teammates and to correct them with appropriate tact and timing. They expect you to have the **TotalCourage!** to be loyal to them and to your team.

The great American philosopher Henry David Thoreau challenged us to lead the life that we imagine and not the life that society or our parents imagine for us. Be loyal; be honest. Never pass a mistake. Be humble. Lift those around you up in the face of adversity. Lead a principled life, lead the life that you imagine, and apply character in all that you see and do.

TOTALCOURAGE! LESSON PLAN & ACTIVITY

Lesson objective:

Guide students to…

- …define the character trait of loyalty.
- …see loyalty in their lives.
- …apply and develop the principle of loyalty personally.
- …engage in both large and small group discussions about loyalty.

1. **Formal *Merriam-Webster* Definition of *Loyalty***
   Loyalty: a loyal feeling: a feeling of strong support for someone or something.
2. **TotalCourage! Definition of *Loyalty*:**
   Loyalty means being true and faithful to your organization, your team, your coaches, and your teammates, but not always in that order.
3. **Please provide your personal definition of *loyalty*:**

_____

_____

_____

4. Case Presentation

The following is an another account from Dee.

"In late 2003 I witnessed an act of loyalty that will stick with me for the rest of my life. On a resupply convoy north of Baghdad, one of my units was hit by an ambush. The unit fought through the ambush by using one of our four battle drills. A battle drill is a rehearsed set of individual and collective tasks to accomplish a tactical mission. A battle drill is just like a "play" drawn up by coaches for football, basketball, soccer, lacrosse, or hockey. One of the most respected leaders in that unit was a sergeant from Alabama. His name was Sgt. Rodriguez*. When the convoy was initially hit by an improvised explosive device or IED, which triggered the ambush, Sgt. Rodriguez was hit in the left arm because he was driving with his right hand and his left arm was resting on the door to capture more air in the cab because of the intense heat. His arm was shredded by shrapnel. After the enemy was defeated and the unit was consolidating and reorganizing to continue the mission, our medics patched him up. They offered to medevac him back to my battalion headquarters in Nasiriyah, where I had a surgeon and a medical aid station set up in an old blown-up building. He declined the offer and continued the mission. After delivering the vital supplies to forward-deployed units, the convoy was ambushed again on the way back home. This time Sgt. Rodriguez was riding in a gun truck because the medics thought it would be more comfortable in that vehicle. Subsequently, he was wounded again. Upon return to my headquarters, and before going to the aid station, he sought me out to apologize for getting wounded in the likelihood that he would be evacuated for medical treatment, thus being unavailable to lead his troops. His loyalty to his soldiers and his team were unequaled that day. I remember writing a letter to his wife in 140-degree heat in the middle of a sandstorm reminding her of his **TotalCourage!**, loyalty, and commitment."

*Name altered for confidentiality purposes.

5. **Small-Group Breakout Session**
   Please pair up and interview your partner asking the following questions.

   The **TotalCourage! Institute** believes that being true to and supporting those around you can only happen in a climate of mutual respect and trust. How did Sgt. Rodriguez demonstrate a climate of mutual respect and trust for his teammates and commanders?

   _____

   _____

   _____

   _____

   Does your team foster a climate of mutual respect and trust? Please describe below how your team does/does not combat a climate of selfishness, lies, and bad behavior.

   _____

   _____

   _____

   _____

6. **Group Discussion: Let's talk collectively about your team's climate.**

   Please use the space below to write down your team's goals and leadership philosophy.

   Goals:

   _____

   _____

   _____

   _____

   Leadership Philosophy:

   _____

   _____

   _____

   _____

   While maintaining honesty and being respectful and supportive of your coach's goals and leadership philosophy, how do you intend to be **loyal** to your team and mentor your teammates with appropriate tact and timing?

   _____

   _____

   _____

   _____

TOTALCOURAGE! JOURNAL

Please answer the following questions prior to our next session. This journal entry will serve as a reminder of how to live a life of loyalty and ultimately a life based on **TotalCourage!**

Throughout our lesson on loyalty we discussed the formal and **TotalCourage!** definitions. You developed your personal definition, and we collectively discussed your team's goals and philosophy. Use the space below to develop your own quote. Write your quote down, put it in a place that will serve as a daily reminder, and be sure to foster a climate of respect and trust. You are encouraged to continue using social media as a platform to spread your positive message; share your quote with others!

"

"

—_____

Social Media Suggestion
Those who wish to use social media instead of writing in a journal can tweet or post their thoughts to **@totalcourage** using the hashtag *#loyalty*.

10

Emotional Maturity

Understanding and managing your emotions

We have covered a lot of territory as we define what **TotalCourage!** really means. Leading a principled life is the greatest single investment you can make. Hopefully, you are applying the previous character traits that are essential to leading a life that you imagine.

Now is the perfect time to discuss emotional maturity. It is one of the toughest character traits to master, and it takes a lifetime of work, reflection, and reinforcement. Remember, we agreed that your reputation is what other people think about you, but character is who you are when no one else is looking.

As an athlete and a teammate, you will be faced with adversity. Your emotional maturity will determine how well you cope with adversity. It is the ability to understand and manage your emotions in both victory and defeat. A champion is resilient, humble, and positive. A champion is responsible, calm, flexible, and nonjudgmental. These are the ingredients of emotional maturity.

Setbacks and adversity are unavoidable in life. Face your challenges with dignity, learn from your mistakes, and then move on. The train of life has left the station, and you are rolling down the track. Face life responsibly, and have a sense of humor. Learn to laugh at yourself and enjoy the fellowship of being a mature and responsible leader among your peers. Be confident. The next play or the next day is a new start.

Learn and grow! Excel and enjoy the journey.

TOTALCOURAGE! LESSON PLAN & ACTIVITY

Lesson objective:

Guide students to…

- …define the character trait of emotional maturity.
- …see emotional maturity in their lives.
- …apply and develop the principle of emotional maturity personally.
- …engage in both large- and small-group discussions about emotional maturity.

1. **TotalCourage! Definition of *Emotional Maturity***
   Your emotional maturity will determine how well you cope with adversity. It is the ability to understand and manage your emotions in both victory and defeat.

2. **Please provide your personal definition of *emotional maturity*:**

_____

_____

_____

3. Case Presentation

The following case presentation is an excerpt from an article written by Jon Paul Morosi and published online by Fox Sports on October 15, 2015.

While reading the excerpt, please consider the themes we have discussed regarding emotional maturity.

<u>Houston Astros Phenom Carlos Correa Shows Maturity in Loss</u>

Correa's parents, Carlos Sr. and Sandybel, watched the series at home in Puerto Rico, and he spoke with them over the phone afterward, and again Tuesday.

"My dad said, 'That's the man I raised. I'm so proud of you. There was no excuses. There was no blaming anybody. That says a lot about you and the way we raised you,'" Correa said. "He's the guy I look up to, so that made me feel really good."

Correa was the No. 1 overall pick in the 2012 MLB draft, the same year he graduated from the Puerto Rico Baseball Academy. Had he enrolled at a US college, this would be the fall of his senior year. Ask yourself how many undergraduates would have such composure after making a mistake viewed by millions of people.

Correa understands what he represents in a multilingual and multicultural league that is working to strengthen Puerto Rico's talent pipeline and plans to host regular-season games in San Juan next year. He took the initiative to arrange a meeting with MLB commissioner Rob Manfred earlier this year to discuss the next steps in nurturing Puerto Rican baseball. Correa even appointed himself an unofficial recruiter for Puerto Rico's 2017 World Baseball Classic team, saying he'll lobby players like Jake Arrieta, Marcus Stroman, Nolan Arenado, and George Springer, who are eligible to play for Puerto Rico or the US. "George is going to play for us," a grinning Correa said of his Astros teammate.

Correa went zero for three in the Astros' Game 5 loss Wednesday night. He was on deck when their season ended. But he has shown that he *gets it*, and the grace with which he carried himself during a brief turn in the October spotlight ensured that one ground ball won't be the lasting image of his 2015 season. In time, though, the

Astros and many baseball fans around the world will view this taut five-game series for what it was: Carlos Correa's grand arrival to the global baseball stage.

Houston's twenty-one-year-old shortstop phenom batted .350 (7-for-20) in the series and on Monday became the youngest player in AL postseason history with a two-homer game. He did it despite being hit by a 97 mph Yordano Ventura fastball in his first at-bat of Game 4, resulting in a left elbow contusion so severe that he couldn't even button his shirt the next morning. And while he made a crucial error as the Astros collapsed in the eighth inning of the same game, even *that* play underscored what the Astros (and Major League Baseball) have in Correa. As soon as the Astros' clubhouse opened to reporters late Monday afternoon, Correa was at his locker. Immediately, a thicket of cameras and microphones surrounded him. He patiently answered questions in English, then his native Spanish, then English again, then Spanish again. When asked about the two home runs, he said only that they were not enough for the Astros to win. When asked about the error, he took responsibility while projecting calm to nearby teammates still absorbing the loss. He could have focused on how the ball's spin changed twice—once when it glanced off reliever Tony Sipp's glove, and again as it caromed sharply off the back of the mound. He didn't. "I just accept that I missed it," he told me at Kauffman Stadium the next day. "I'm not perfect. I was not frustrated or anything like that. "People say I choked. I didn't choke. You know what? After you hit two home runs, and you have four RBIs, you put your team ahead by three runs, you have the most confidence in the world. You feel like the man. You want the ball hit at you and make a great play and finish your day strong. It wasn't because I was nervous. I wanted the ball hit at me. I wasn't expecting to miss a chopper. But I missed it. It happens. It wasn't meant to be our day."

4. **Individual Exercise**

   Remember, your emotional maturity will determine how well you cope with adversity. It is the ability to understand and manage your emotions in both victory and defeat. A champion is resilient, humble, and positive. A champion is responsible, calm, flexible, and nonjudgmental. These are the ingredients of emotional maturity.

   Please dissect the case example above and identify at least three **TotalCourage!** ingredients of emotional maturity that are present throughout the case example.

   1. _____

      _____

      _____

   2. _____

      _____

      _____

   3. _____

      _____

      _____

5. **Group Discussion**

   Reflecting on your individual exercise, please share with the group what you have identified as examples of ingredients of emotional maturity. As a group, we will identify our top three ingredients of emotional maturity that lead to being a mature and responsible leader among your peers.

   1. _____

      _____

      _____

      _____

   2. _____

      _____

      _____

      _____

   3. _____

      _____

      _____

      _____

TOTALCOURAGE! JOURNAL

This journal entry will serve as a reminder of how to live a life of emotional maturity and ultimately a life of **TotalCourage!**

How do you want to be remembered? Please use the space below to write your own headline and a paragraph on how you have demonstrated emotional maturity in the face of adversity. Remember, setbacks and adversity are unavoidable in life. Face your challenges with dignity, learn from your mistakes, and then move on.

Article Title:

_____

Article Excerpt:

_____

_____

_____

_____

Social Media Suggestion
Those who wish to use social media instead of writing in a journal can tweet or post their thoughts to **@totalcourage** using the hashtag *#emotionalmaturity*.

11

Gratitude

Gratitude is about attitude.

An inestimable character trait required in order to be a true winner and leader both on the field and off is gratitude. Increasingly, we live in a society in which ordinary individuals and talented athletes have a false sense of entitlement. Do not allow yourself to fall into that trap.

You have unique skills and gifts, talents and willpower to lead the life that you imagine and to be a role model and a champion. The world, the government, your school, your administrators, and your coaches don't owe you anything. Greatness is earned through character and hard work. There are no shortcuts.

A star athlete on a high-profile Division I football team tweeted that playing sports in college is a form of modern slavery. Clearly that comment was out of place. However, the message is that there are athletes who come from all socioeconomic backgrounds, from all parts of the world, who believe that once they are in a privileged situation they are entitled to receive more. Our advice at **TotalCourage!** is to be grateful for the opportunities that lie before you.

Have the **TotalCourage!** to lead a principled life and focus on your character, hard work, and teamwork. Do these things, and the appropriate entitlements will be available to you.

Gratitude is about attitude. A bad attitude only hurts the person with the bad attitude. Be thankful for all the blessings that you have. A positive attitude is infectious. A bad attitude is like a cancer that prevents you from leading a life filled with potential.

Be positive. Be a winner. Be grateful!

TOTALCOURAGE! LESSON PLAN & ACTIVITY
Lesson objective:

Guide students to...

- ...define the character trait of gratitude.
- ...see loyalty in their lives.
- ...apply and develop the principle of gratitude personally.
- ...engage in both large and small group discussions about gratitude.

1. **Formal *Merriam-Webster* Definition of *Gratitude***
   Gratitude: a feeling of appreciation or thanks.
2. **TotalCourage! Definition of *Gratitude***
   Thankfulness for your gifts, talents, and abilities and being responsible in sharing your gifts; remembering to be thankful to those who have helped you along the way. The power of a "thank you" is universal and strengthens your character.
3. **Please provide your personal definition of *gratitude*:**

   _____

   _____

   _____

4. Individual Exercise

Please refer to Chapter 3 for our lesson on integrity. In lesson three you were asked to select one individual who you believe embodies a life based on integrity and provide a description of that individual. This individual could have been a role model, mentor, coach, relative, or public figure. Use the space below to write a note of gratitude to that individual. In your note, focus on expressing a feeling of thanks or appreciation for what they have offered you in your own life. Specifically, speak to how they have assisted you in obtaining the unique skills and gifts, talents and willpower to lead the life that you imagine and to be a role model and a champion.

Dear _____,

_____

_____

_____

_____

_____

_____

_____

_____

_____

_____

5. **Group Discussion**

   Please share with the group why you have chosen to express gratitude to this specific individual and the ways he or she has contributed to molding you as an individual of character to lead a principled life.

   We at **TotalCourage!** understand that the note may be intimate and personal. You do not have to share those thoughts that are most intimate; however, we encourage you to share your thoughts regarding the importance of living a life of gratitude, as this will stimulate learning within the group. Please use the space below to formulate your thoughts or write down any important points that are offered by those in your group.

   My Thoughts:

   _____

   _____

   _____

   _____

   Group Thoughts:

   _____

   _____

   _____

   _____

TOTALCOURAGE! JOURNAL

This journal entry will serve as a reminder of how to live a life of gratitude and ultimately a life based on **TotalCourage!**

We encourage you to share your note of gratitude with the individual it is addressed to for today's individual exercise. Your delivery method can be of your choosing. A few recommendations are to handwrite the letter, send it via e-mail, or use an additional form of technology.

We understand there may be extenuating circumstances, making it impossible to deliver your note of gratitude. If this problem presents itself, think outside the box, perhaps providing the note to a loved one of the individual, letting them know how much the individual has contributed to you leading a principled life.

Please use the space below to write how you decided to share your note of gratitude.

_____

_____

_____

_____

Social Media Suggestion
Those who wish to use social media instead of writing in a journal can tweet or post their thoughts to **@totalcourage** using the hashtag *#gratitude*.

12

Decisiveness

Paralysis through analysis is being indecisive.

Rarely in life will you be afforded the time or the resources to come up with a 100-percent solution pertaining to any problem that you or your teams encounter. In order to lead a life of **TotalCourage!** you must be decisive.

Firmness of purpose only comes from being a good listener and from being aware of your surroundings at all times. Train yourself to quickly assess the facts bearing on any problem, determine the assumptions bearing on the problem, and then define two or three ways to solve the problem given the time, resources, and costs as your basic evaluation criteria.

Let's consider the following example:

It is second down and goal from the four-yard line. There are twenty seconds left in the game and the opponent is winning thirty-one to twenty-four. These are your facts bearing on the problem. Of course, the problem is pretty obvious. If your team doesn't score a touchdown and convert the extra point within the next twenty seconds, you lose. Assumptions bearing on the problem are that your opponent expects you to pass in the corner of the end zone because you have exploited their cornerbacks the entire game, and they will most likely pressure your quarterback. Your evaluation criteria are time, resources, and costs. You have the resources to either spread the field and go with what has been successful with the short pass in the flats, or you can go to your goal line offense with an experienced fullback and running back, and the cost (or the risk) of proper clock management can deny you three opportunities to score. Your best options are to exploit the corner of the end zone or do a play-action hand-off to the running back for second down.

What would you do? Be decisive. Be firm of purpose, and if you don't score, no problem! You have two more plays to conduct a quick-decision matrix in your head because you know how to quickly define the problem, the facts bearing on the problem, and the assumptions bearing on the problem.

Remember, you're never alone when making a decision. There is a solution to every problem. The right solution is found by assessing the people, time, resources, and costs/risks associated with the problem. Train your mind through silent drills regarding the smallest problems you face with this time-tested and proven technique, and you will emerge as a decisive teammate and leader.

In the military, we have an old saying that in combat there is only the, "quick and the dead." Good leaders empower their teammates to be decisive by giving them clear intent regarding the problem that must be solved and providing them with the right resources.

In sports, business, and for all practical matters in life, those who are decisive win. Those who are disorganized in their thinking, unaware of their surroundings, don't listen, and don't analyze the problem find themselves uncertain, indecisive, and unsuccessful.

Remember that paralysis through analysis is being indecisive. Do your best to get that 90-percent solution and make a decision. Analyze, but don't overanalyze. Refine your decisions along the way.

Be decisive!

TOTALCOURAGE! LESSON PLAN & ACTIVITY
Lesson objective:

Guide students to...

- ...define the character trait of decisiveness.
- ...see decisiveness in their lives.
- ...apply and develop the principle of decisiveness personally.
- ...engage in both large and small group discussions about decisiveness.

1. **Formal *Merriam-Webster* Definition of *Decisiveness***
   Decisiveness:
   - ability to make choices quickly and confidently.
   - clarity and obviousness.
2. **TotalCourage! Definition of *Decisiveness***
   The ability to make well-informed decisions in a timely manner.
3. **Please provide your personal definition of *decisiveness*:**

_____

_____

_____

4. Case Example and Small-Group Breakout Session

Decision making is all about defining the problem, determining the facts and assumptions bearing on the problem, and developing courses of action to solve the problem. True decisiveness is not waiting around for the 100-percent solution. Strive for the 90-percent solution, and refine your decision along the way. Decisiveness requires initiative, knowledge, and resourcefulness. In order to be decisive, you must train yourself to be a good listener, and you must die to your ego in order to combine ideas and best practices from others. If you're in charge as the captain of your team, as the coach on the sideline, or the businessman or woman closing a sale, be decisive.

Please read the problem presented below and work closely with your partner to respond to the corresponding statements below the case example. You have seven minutes to complete the exercise.

> Cole, a Division I student-athlete, was at a downtown bar with several of his friends during the offseason. Cole had witnessed several of his teammates appearing to become intoxicated. As he witnessed his teammates increase their alcohol consumption, he also witnessed them making sexual gestures toward several women at the bar. At first it seemed friendly, but then he noticed the women beginning to become agitated. He did not witness any physical contact of a sexual nature; however, he overheard two teammates making sexual comments to the women. Cole believed the comments and gestures to be highly offensive. He decided not to engage in the conversation, as he did not want to offend his teammates or be a part of the conversation. Cole decided to leave the bar with one of his teammates. The next morning, several of his teammates were called into the head coach's office. A video had surfaced on social media of his teammates making the explicitly sexual comments, and an article was published in the school newspaper. Cole was not called into the office, nor was he in the video. This incident quickly put a black eye on the Division I program.

Define the problem:

_____

_____

_____

Determine the facts and assumptions bearing on the problem:

_____

_____

_____

Develop courses of action to solve the problem:

_____

_____

_____

90-percent solution:

_____

_____

_____

6. Group Discussion

Good leaders empower their teammates to be decisive by giving them clear intent on the problem that must be solved and providing them with the right resources. We will elicit feedback from the teams on the questions below.

How was the process of working together to determine the facts and assumptions bearing on the problem?

_____

_____

_____

Did your group develop courses of action to solve the problem in a timely manner?

_____

_____

_____

Were you a good listener and did you work together to combine ideas and best practices to formulate a 90-percent solution?

_____

_____

_____

TOTALCOURAGE! JOURNAL

This journal entry will serve as a reminder of the importance of being decisive in your daily life and ultimately living a life of **TotalCourage!**

Decisions! Decisions! Decisions! Remember, you're never alone when making a decision. Training yourself to be a good listener requires a conscious effort on a daily basis. Before we start our next lesson, provide at least one example of how you were a good listener, died to your ego, and combined your ideas and best practices from others to form a decisive result for the betterment of those around you.

Real-Life Example:

_____

_____

_____

_____

_____

_____

_____

_____

Social Media Suggestion
Those who wish to use social media instead of writing in a journal can tweet or post their thoughts to **@totalcourage** using the hashtag *#decisiveness*.

13

Resilience

Find the perfect human being and you will find in that person the perfect imposter.

Regardless of your socioeconomic background, your race, your faith, your abilities, or your skills, you will face obstacles in life. Symbolically, you will be knocked down. The measure of a person is not how fast they get back up when knocked down but the manner in which they get back up. Sometimes in life we try to attack the hill, and it is steep and loaded with landmines.

Time heals. However, you can compress the healing time by the way that you act. Sometimes you can go around the hill and bypass it altogether. Sometimes it's better to not even try to attack the hill and save it for another day or another time in your life. We all make mistakes. We are all fraught with human frailty. Mitigate the pain in your life by making well-informed decisions. You're not in this life alone.

There is no problem that cannot be solved! Resilience means to bounce back from adversity. Oftentimes, adversity is unavoidable, but most of the time, with proper planning, sound decision making, and the help of others, adversity can be avoided.

Life is really about expectation management. It is important to have goals and to have a dream that is bigger than yourself. However, "Rome was not built in a day." If life were easy, everybody would be a millionaire, and think about how boring that would be! Your life will involve challenges, and if you look at these challenges as opportunities rather than obstacles, your chance of success increases exponentially.

Resilience is about attitude. Let the negative roll off your back like water off a duck. Don't get mad; don't get even; just get what you want by leading a life of confidence, patience, and integrity. Remember, we see the past as history. We learn from the past, but we don't dwell on the past. Seize the day! Get back up with character; don't make excuses, and keep striving to lead the life that you imagine.

Be resilient!

TOTALCOURAGE! LESSON PLAN & ACTIVITY
Lesson objective:

Guide students to…

- …define the character trait of resilience.
- …see resilience in their lives.
- …apply and develop the principle of resilience personally.
- …engage in both large and small group discussions about resilience.

1. **Formal *Merriam-Webster* Definition of *Resilience***
   Resilience: the ability to become strong, healthy, or successful again after something bad happens.

2. **TotalCourage! Definition of *Resilience***
   Resilience is the ability to bounce back from adversity with character!

3. **Please provide your personal definition of *resilience*:**

   _____

   _____

   _____

4. Case Presentation

For this next presentation, we will present a film: *BOATLIFT, An Untold Tale of 9/11 Resilience.* Tom Hanks narrates the epic story of 9/11 boatlift that evacuated half a million people from the stricken piers and seawalls of Lower Manhattan.

Please go to the following link (under 12 minutes):

https://www.youtube.com/watch?v=MDOrzF7B2Kg

5. Group Discussion

As stated above, we at **TotalCourage!** believe that resilience is about attitude. Let the negative roll off your back like water off a duck. Don't get mad; don't get even; just get what you want by leading a life of confidence, patience, and integrity.

How did the individuals featured in this film lead a life of confidence, patience, and integrity while faced with incomprehensible adversity?

_____

_____

_____

How can we as a team learn from the experiences of those in the film *BOATLIFT* and examine our challenges as opportunities rather than obstacles?

_____

_____

_____

TOTALCOURAGE! JOURNAL

This journal entry will serve as a reminder of how to live a life of resilience and ultimately a life based on **TotalCourage!**

In our final lesson you will be asked to live your story and write your own chapter. As we have discussed throughout this lesson on resilience, life is really about expectation management. It is important to have goals and to have a dream that is bigger than yourself. Take some time to reflect on our previous lessons and identify your expectations and goals. List them below as this will assist you in brainstorming ways to write your own chapter!

_____

_____

_____

_____

_____

_____

_____

Social Media Suggestion
Those who wish to use social media instead of writing in a journal can tweet or post their thoughts to **@totalcourage** using the hashtag *#resilience*.

14

Live Your Story

Your life is an open book! Our stories are very personal but our stories are also very transparent. Social media and society require us to write a story of our lives that is, above all things, true to oneself. If we lead our lives above reproach, then our story becomes our distinct brand with its own unique set of experiences, achievements, relationships, and messages of hope and humility.

After all, isn't hope the confident expectation that something good is going to happen? Isn't humility about quiet, caring selflessness? Parents and guardians, mentors, teachers, coaches, friends, public figures, and historical figures all shape our character. Our faith shapes our character.

However, there is only one author of your life story. YOU! Your life story does not have to be perfect nor does it have to be exhilarating like a Jason Bourne movie, but it can be an inspiration to those you may never even meet in person.

You are living in the most knowledgeable generation in the history of mankind because you and your peers have a smartphone at your disposal 24/7. Instantly, you can reach back and quickly grasp any fact, assumption, or research from the past or the present. So with this powerful tool, what differentiates you from everyone else? What makes your story so interesting? Well, it is character. It is having the **TotalCourage!** to win with character every single day of your life. You set yourself apart when you lead a life of transparency and integrity and when you lend a helping hand to those who may not have the privileges that you have or the skills and abilities that you have.

Brand yourself as something bigger than any dollar amount could ever endorse. Do the right thing, and do things right. Remember, your generation is the first true generation in global society whereupon the entire world has the ability to watch, and to know, what you are doing, how you're behaving, and what you are thinking.

Your legacy will be indelibly digitized in social media and on the Internet for generations to come. Be remembered as a role model and not a coward. As we have discussed in previous lessons, it takes a person of **TotalCourage!** to lead a principled life and a coward to lead a life of selfishness, indiscipline, and immorality. Live your story!

Wrap the present with a great big bow and give yourself the gift of a powerful brand as you write the story of your life. Your life story matters regardless of your race, your faith, your skills or your abilities because you are unique, and you bring skill sets and viewpoints that are entirely your own.

Write a story that your grandchildren and great grandchildren will be proud of when you have crossed the river and the last chapter is written.

Your life story is your legacy.

TOTALCOURAGE! LESSON PLAN & ACTIVITY
Lesson objective:

Guide students to…

- …conceptualize their own life story.
- …apply their own life story and develop their own **TotalCourage!** character trait, lesson plan, and journal entry.

1. **Individual Exercise**
   Please use the template below to develop your own **TotalCourage!** chapter. Your life story and feedback is invaluable to the **TotalCourage!** team.

   By no means does the ***TotalCourage!** Institute Playbook* contain an exhaustive list of character traits.

   By completing your own chapter you will not only help yourself lead a principled life, but you will also assist the **TotalCourage!** team in developing future and extended versions of the playbook. You just may see YOUR chapter in our next edition!

WRITE YOUR OWN CHAPTER

Chapter 15: _____

" " " "

1. **Formal _Merriam-Webster_ Definition of** _____

   _____: _____

   : _____

2. **TotalCourage! Definition of** _____

   _____

3. **Please provide your personal definition of** _____:

   _____

   _____

   _____

4. **Case Presentation**

(Please use the space below to complete your case example or presentation for your own character trait.)

5. **Small-Group Breakout Discussion** (Use the space below to list questions or statements to assist in facilitating a small-group discussion about your character trait and case presentation.)

_____

_____

_____

_____

_____

_____

_____

_____

TOTALCOURAGE! JOURNAL

This journal entry will serve as a reminder of how to live a life of _____ and ultimately a life of **TotalCourage!**

(Please list journal questions or activities for your character trait in the space below.)

_____

_____

_____

_____

_____

_____

_____

Social Media Suggestion
Those who wish to use social media instead of writing in a journal can tweet or post their thoughts to **@totalcourage** using the hashtag
#_____.

Epilogue

TotalCourage! is about winning with character! This curriculum represents a fresh and dynamic approach. The intent is to provide a foundation of character to our current and future generations of student-athletes.

In past generations, education was a key differentiator in a society where the majority of people had a strong foundation of character traits instilled in them by their parents, teachers, and religious leaders. Those previous generations were held accountable, and it was a common denominator.

Paradoxically, today's youth have an opportunity to differentiate themselves from a society where knowledge, regardless of the quality of their public or private education, is at their fingertips 24/7 with access to smartphones, tablets, and computers. Knowledge today is universal. Character, unfortunately, is not.

How can coaches differentiate themselves from all of the other coaches in a competitive environment in which coaching clinics and other resources share plays, strategies, techniques, and methodologies for all to implement? The answer is character!

How can student-athletes differentiate themselves on the field and off the field? Our youth today have unbelievable pressure to conform to the messages in popular culture. In music, attire, jewelry, and on film, it is cool to imitate gang or immoral behavior.

The reward in life is in the finish. If you want to finish strong you must differentiate yourself from others, and the secret sauce is character. This first edition is a living document, and it will get stronger as we take this path of learning and experience together.

Write your own exciting life story! Create your own unique brand, differentiate yourself, and win with character. The rewards will fall into your lap when you least expect them. It is truly the quintessential gift that keeps on giving.

Please reach out to us and share your journey and let others know the value of leading a principled life!

About the Authors

DEE DAUGHERTY

Colonel, US Army (retired)

TotalCourage! Executive Director

Dee is a proven combat leader with over thirty-two years of experience creating winning teams. Dee was an honor graduate of the US Army Airborne School, French Commando School, US Marine Corps Amphibious Warfare School, and the Defense Language Institute. He received his MS from National Defense University in National Resource Strategy. Inducted into the US Army Officers Candidate School Hall of Fame, Dee started his career as an enlisted infantryman. As a senior officer, Dee developed and executed plans for large and complex humanitarian and combat operations worldwide. Dee is the founder of **TotalCourage!**

KENNETH MARFILIUS, LCSW

TotalCourage! Coauthor

Ken is a proven leader in the academic, athletic, and military arenas. Ken was a student athlete at Syracuse University, where he excelled in both the classroom and in Division I athletics. He completed his undergraduate studies at Syracuse University, and he received his master's degree from the University of Pennsylvania. While at Penn, Ken worked with our nation's veterans and was selected for a US Air Force Health Professions Scholarship. As a result, Ken received a direct commission in the US Air Force and managed AF mental health programs. Ken is currently a doctoral candidate at the University of Pennsylvania.

Coaches and Advisers

Our coaching team has over 125 years of combined experience training and mentoring thousands of young men and women to lead their own lives with character. Some coaches are National Association of Collegiate Directors of Athletics (NACDA), National Association of Compliance (NAAC) members, and Certified NCAA DI Compliance Coordinators. We understand the by-laws and the value of playing by the rules! You can learn more about our coaches and who they are on our website www.totalcourage.org.

TotalCourage! has established a world class Advisory Council to act as ambassadors for **TotalCourage!** and to use their influence to open doors for our character coaches. The Advisory Council also helps identify fund-raising opportunities and provides guidance to our strategic planning process. You can meet and learn more about our Advisory Council and who they are on our website, www.totalcourage.org.

Support Us

TotalCourage! assists schools, coaches, and athletes with proven tools to win with character. Our services are free to these school, coaches, and athletes. We need your help to provide these services. We ask you to join our mission, understanding that every donation helps us teach your young men and women how to lead a principled life. Help us in our quest to create leaders of tomorrow who can excel in the face of adversity. Help these young athletes lead a life of limitless possibilities, happiness, and confidence…a life of **TotalCourage!**

Your donation can be made online at:

http://www.totalcourage.org/support-us.html

Or by mail, addressed to:

TOTAL COURAGE INC.
5201 KINGSTON PIKE STE 6–322
KNOXVILLE, TN 37919

TotalCourage! is a qualified 501(c)(3) tax-exempt organization. Your donations are tax deductible to the fullest extent of the law. Please contact your tax adviser for additional information.

Follow us on social media **@totalcourage**.

Recommended Reading List

Aurelius, Marcus. *Meditations*. New York, NY: Penguin Group, 2005.

Bell, Rob. *How to Be Here.* New York, NY: HarperCollins Publishers, 2016.

Dow, Philip E. *Virtuous Minds: Intellectual Character Development*. Downers Grove, IL: IVP Academic, 2013.

Holtz, Lou. *Winning Every Day: The Game Plan for Success.* New York, NY:

HarperCollins Publishers, 1998.

Puryear, Edgar. *Nineteen Stars: A Study in Military Character and Leadership.*

New York, NY: Random House Publishing Group, 1993.

Schultz, Howard & Chandrasekaran, Rajiv. *For Love of Country: What Our Veterans Can Teach Us about Citizenship, Heroism, and Sacrifice.* New York, NY: Alfred A. Knopf, 2014.

References

"BOATLIFT, An Untold Tale of 9/11 Resilience," YouTube video, 11:56, posted by www.road2resilience.com, September 7, 2011, https://www.youtube.com/watch?v=MDOrzF7B2Kg.

Morosi, Jon Paul, "Houston Astros Phenom Carlos Correa Shows Maturity in Loss." *Fox Sports,* last modified October 15, 2015, http://www.foxsports.com/mlb/story/houston-astros-phenom-carlos-correa-shows-maturity-in-loss-101515.

Merriam-Webster.com, s.v. "commitment," accessed April 19, 2016, http://www.merriam-webster.com/dictionary/commitment.

Merriam-Webster.com, s.v. "decisiveness," accessed April 16, 2016, http://www.merriam-webster.com/dictionary/decisiveness.

Merriam-Webster.com, s.v. "diplomacy," accessed April 17, 2016, http://www.merriam-webster.com/dictionary/diplomacy.

Merriam-Webster.com, s.v. "enthusiasm," accessed April 21, 2016, http://www.merriam-webster.com/dictionary/enthusiasm.

Merriam-Webster.com, s.v. "gratitude," accessed April 17, 2016, http://www.merriam-webster.com/dictionary/gratitude.

Merriam-Webster.com, s.v. "humility," accessed April 17, 2016, http://www.merriam-webster.com/dictionary/humility.

Merriam-Webster.com, s.v. "initiative," accessed April 18, 2016, http://www.merriam-webster.com/dictionary/initiative.

Merriam-Webster.com, s.v. "integrity," accessed April 18, 2016, http://www.merriam-webster.com/dictionary/integrity.

Merriam-Webster.com, s.v. "loyalty," accessed April 15, 2016, http://www.merriam-webster.com/dictionary/loyalty.

Merriam-Webster.com, s.v. "resilience," accessed April 19, 2016, http://www.merriam-webster.com/dictionary/resilience.

Merriam-Webster.com, s.v. "selflessness," accessed April 15, 2016, http://www.merriam-webster.com/dictionary/selflessness.

Merriam-Webster.com, s.v. "tact," accessed April 14, 2016, http://www.merriam-webster.com/dictionary/tact.

"30 for 30 Shorts: Student Athlete," YouTube video, 13:32, posted by SportsToday, January 14, 2015, http://www.youtube.com/watch?v=makDyycHvmw&feature=fvhl.